LEXINGTON PUBLIC LIBRARY

MY FRIENDS SPREAD A RUMOR

WORKING IT OUT

You Choose the Ending

by Connie Colwell Miller • illustrated by Sofia Cardoso

Do you ever wish you could change a story or choose a different ending?

IN THESE BOOKS, YOU CAN!

Read along and when you see this:

WHAT HAPPENS NEXT?

Skip to the page for that choice, and see what happens.

In this story, Harper's friends spread a rumor about her. Will she work out the problem, or will she let it go?
YOU make the choices!

"Hey, Harper," Danny says, "I heard you wet the bed."
Harper turns red. "Where did you hear that?" she demands.
"Natalie and Hadleigh told us," Jay says. Natalie and Hadleigh are supposed to be Harper's friends!

WHAT HAPPENS NEXT?

If Harper doesn't say anything to her friends, turn the page.
If Harper talks to her friends right away, turn to page 20.

Harper's friends join her at lunch. She says nothing. She can feel herself getting angrier and angrier. She wonders how her friends could spread such an untrue rumor.

"What's up, Harper?" Natalie says.

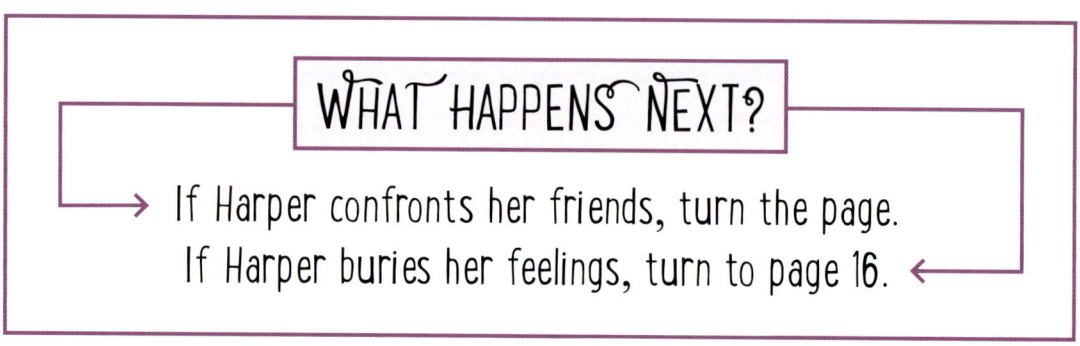

WHAT HAPPENS NEXT?

If Harper confronts her friends, turn the page.
If Harper buries her feelings, turn to page 16.

5

Harper decides to say something.

"I know you've been spreading a rumor about me. How could you? You're supposed to be my friends!"

Natalie and Hadleigh look surprised and ashamed.

TURN TO PAGE 18 →

Harper stands up. Tears roll down her cheeks.

"You're supposed to be my friends, but you spread rumors about me!" she shouts at the girls. "I hate you!"

Her friends look up in shock.

TURN THE PAGE →

The girls start arguing.
"Jeez, we only did it once," Hadleigh says.
"Yeah, it was just a joke," Natalie says.

Harper leaves the lunchroom angry and upset. She doesn't want to be friends with Natalie and Hadleigh anymore.

THE END
→ Go to page 23.

Harper picks at her food and says nothing to her friends. When lunch finally ends, Natalie and Hadleigh skip off to the playground together. They look back at Harper, but she doesn't look like she wants to play with them.

Harper's anger hardens over several days. She avoids her friends until they stop asking her to play.

The rumor dies out. She wishes she had told her friends how she felt. She decides that when she makes new friends, she will be more open about her feelings.

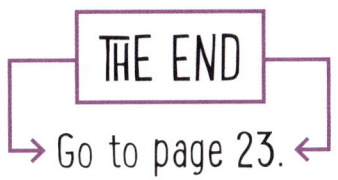

THE END

Go to page 23.

Harper ignores Natalie. Natalie shrugs and turns to chat with Hadleigh instead.

Harper can feel tears stinging the backs of her eyes.

WHAT HAPPENS NEXT?

If Harper gets angry, turn to page 8.
If Harper holds back her tears, turn to page 12.

"We're sorry, Harper," Natalie says. "We didn't think about your feelings."

"Can you forgive us?" asks Hadleigh.

Harper's anger softens a bit. "I need some cool-off time," she says. Harper knows she will forgive her friends after a while, after the rumor dies out.

THE END
↳ Go to page 23. ←

Harper approaches her friends at lunch. She tries to stay calm.

"Hi," she says. "I know you two have been spreading untrue rumors about me. It hurts my feelings, and I want you to stop."

"We're sorry," Natalie says. "We thought it was funny."
"We'll stop," says Hadleigh.
After a few days, the rumor dies down. Harper forgives her friends. She's glad she told them how she felt.

THE END

THINK AGAIN

- What happened at the end of the path you chose?
- Did you like that ending?
- Go back to page 3. Read the story again and pick different choices. How did the story change?

We all can choose what to do when people hurt us. If your friend spread rumors about you, would YOU speak up, or would you let it go?

For my dearest friend Deborah and her lovely granddaughters—C.C.M.

AMICUS ILLUSTRATED is published by Amicus
P.O. Box 227, Mankato, MN 56002
www.amicuspublishing.us

© 2023 Amicus. International copyright reserved in all countries. No part of this book may be reproduced in any form without written permission from the publisher.

Library of Congress Cataloging-in-Publication Data
Names: Miller, Connie Colwell, 1976- author. | Cardoso, Sofia (Illustrator), illustrator.
Title: My friends spread a rumor : working it out : you choose the ending / by Connie Colwell Miller ; illustrated by Sofia Cardoso.
Description: Mankato, MN : Amicus, [2023] | Series: Making good choices | Audience: Ages 6-9 | Audience: Grades 2-3 | Summary: "In this illustrated choose-your-own-ending picture book, Harper's friends spread a rumor that she wets the bed. Will Harper confront them or let it go? Will she forgive her friends? Readers make choices for Harper and read what happens next, with each story path leading to different outcomes. Includes four different endings and discussion questions."—Provided by publisher.
Identifiers: LCCN 2021057141 (print) | LCCN 2021057142 (ebook) | ISBN 9781645492757 (hardcover) | ISBN 9781681527994 (paperback) | ISBN 9781645493631 (ebook)
Subjects: LCSH: Truthfulness and falsehood in children--Juvenile literature. | Rumor--Juvenile literature. | Friendship in children--Juvenile literature.
Classification: LCC BF723.T8 M548 2023 (print) | LCC BF723.T8 (ebook) | DDC 177/.3083--dc23/eng/20211221
LC record available at https://lccn.loc.gov/2021057141
LC ebook record available at https://lccn.loc.gov/2021057142

Editor: Rebecca Glaser
Series Designer: Kathleen Petelinsek
Book Designer: Catherine Berthiaume

ABOUT THE AUTHOR

Connie Colwell Miller is a writer, editor, and instructor who lives in Le Sueur, Minnesota, with her four children. She has written over 100 books for young children. She likes to tell stories to her kids to teach them important life lessons.

ABOUT THE ILLUSTRATOR

Sofia Cardoso is a Portuguese children's book illustrator, designer, and foodie, whose passion for illustration goes all the way back to her childhood years. Using a mix of both traditional and digital methods, she now spends her days creating whimsical illustrations, full of color and young characters that aim to inspire joy and creativity in both kids and kids at heart.